Dorothy Dandridge: The Life and Legacy of One of Hollywood's First Successful Black Actresses

By Charles River Editors

About Charles River Editors

Charles River Editors is a boutique digital publishing company, specializing in bringing history back to life with educational and engaging books on a wide range of topics. Keep up to date with our new and free offerings with this 5 second sign up on our weekly mailing list, and visit Our Kindle Author Page to see other recently published Kindle titles.

We make these books for you and always want to know our readers' opinions, so we encourage you to leave reviews and look forward to publishing new and exciting titles each week.

Introduction

"If I were white, I could capture the world." – Dorothy Dandridge

The bright summer sun shined blissfully on a secluded valley tucked into the romantic Costa del Sol in southern Spain. Water bubbled friskily over a rocky streambed as trees swayed in the gentle tropical breeze and dappled the banks in playful shadows. A closer look reveals a man and a woman entwined on the rocky shore in an intimate embrace. The man trembles with longing as he bends over the woman, his parted lips just inches from hers. She eagerly folds her arms around him, her fingertips passionately digging into the skin on his back as she draws him closer.

Suddenly, a director's voice rings out, "Cut!"[1]

The man was white. The woman was black, and in Hollywood in 1959, that was still taboo.

The steamy scene was being shot for the film *Malaga*, and the actress in the scene, Dorothy Dandridge, had just shared Hollywood's controversial first interracial kiss on screen a year earlier.[2] Despite this distinction and other more notable accomplishments, many people today are not familiar with the groundbreaking actress, even as she was among the most charismatic and beautiful actresses of the era. Her alluring nightclub acts set pulses pounding across the globe, and she was Hollywood's first black leading actress.

---

[1] Based on Dorothy Dandridge and Earl Conrad, Earl, *Everything and Nothing: The Dorothy Dandridge Tragedy* (New York: HarperCollins Publishers, 2000 [1970]), 202-203; and Donald Bogle, *Dorothy Dandridge: A Biography* (New York: Amistad Press, Inc., 1997), 435-447.

[2] Bogle, 404 (white actor Stuart Whitman kissed Dorothy in *The Decks Ran Red*).

Sadly, all of it came at a high price. Dorothy bore the scars of a tormented childhood, endured the fallout from multiple failed relationships, suffered professional and financial setbacks, and battled ongoing alcohol and prescription drug abuse. Throughout all that, racism was the most tenacious demon she had to fight, because Dorothy came of age in an era when society and the entertainment world largely held to demeaning racial stereotypes. Though she appeared in 15 movies, her career was overshadowed by the work of contemporary white screen legends such as Grace Kelly, Judy Garland, and Marilyn Monroe. Dorothy understandably believed she could have become so much more if she had been born white. As she poignantly put it, "What was I? That outdated 'tragic mulatto' of earlier fiction? Oddly enough, there remains some validity in this concept, in a society not yet integrated. I wasn't fully accepted in either world, black or white. I was too light to satisfy Negroes, not light enough to secure the screen work, the roles, the marriage status available to a white woman."[3]

Nevertheless, Dorothy made great strides for the black community and blazed trails for minority entertainers. She confronted racial stereotypes, overcame prevailing cinematic conventions, and set attendance records throughout her entire career. She attained genuine stardom as the lead in the 1954 film *Carmen Jones*, and her portrayal earned her an Academy Award nomination for Best Actress, the first such Oscar nod for a black woman.

Dorothy Dandridge: The Life and Legacy of One of Hollywood's First Successful Black Actresses profiles the arduous rise and abrupt fall of Dorothy's radiant stardom. Along with pictures depicting important people, places, and events, you will learn about Dorothy Dandridge like never before.

---

[3] Dandridge and Conrad, 164-165.

The Wonder Children

"To wind one's way sinuously from the most tenuous Cleveland ghetto origin into the labyrinths of our day's concept of 'success'; to feel stardom, love, excitement, triumph; then to spill headlong down into caverns of self-recrimination and inward loathing—it is an odyssey that should be told from the beginning." - Dorothy Dandridge[4]

Dorothy Dandridge's life seemed destined to play out in front of an audience. Dorothy's mother Ruby naturally possessed a flair for the dramatic and learned to sing, dance, and perform acrobatics as a young child, while her father Cyril was handsome, sensitive, unassuming, and content with his middle-class lot in life. Cyril was an only child and doted on his mother, especially after his father died, but while Cyril's and Ruby's personalities were a study in contrasts, they had mixed racial heritage in common.[5] Cyril was half-white, half-black, and Ruby claimed Jamaican, Native American, Hispanic, and white ancestry.[6] Since they were both part black, it was convenient for society to compartmentalize them as "Negro."

After Cyril and Ruby married in September 1919 in their hometown of Cleveland, Ohio, they moved in with Cyril's mother there.[7] The relationships among them were strained from the very start and were further complicated by the birth of Cyril and Ruby's first daughter, Vivian Alfretta, in April 1921. Desiring adventure and longing to perform, Ruby packed up two-month-old Vivian and left. She returned after six weeks, and though the couple attempted to reconcile, Ruby left again in July 1922. This second time, despite being pregnant again, she meant it.

Ruby and Cyril's second baby daughter was born on November 9, 1922. Ruby chose to name her baby Dorothy, a simple, elegant name she felt would be perfect for a movie marquee.[8] Due to her mixed racial heritage, the baby had a light complexion.

Though Ruby stayed in Cleveland, it took Cyril months to locate his family. He pleaded with her to return, but she would not.[9] She erased their father from her daughters' lives and later lied to them, telling the girls that their father had no interest in them. At one point, she even told them he had died. She also cut ties with her extended family. Ruby won a court settlement against Cyril for a $10 monthly child support payment, and even though he still desired to reconcile, he filed for divorce in June 1924. Years of contentious legal and custody battles followed.

All the while, Ruby needed to support her family, so she worked days as kitchen help and

---

[4] Ibid., 11.

[5] Bogle, 4-6

[6] Earl Mills, *Dorothy Dandridge: An Intimate Biography of Hollywood's First Major Black Film Star*, 1999 ed. (Los Angeles: Holloway House Publishing Company, 1970), 106.

[7] Bogle, 7.

[8] Ibid., 9.

[9] Ibid., 9.

danced, sang, and recited poetry at local church gatherings on evenings and weekends when time allowed. Young Dorothy was mesmerized by her mother's rehearsals and absorbed every detail. Dorothy made her public performance debut when Ruby came home from work too tired to fulfill an engagement scheduled for later that evening. When Dorothy offered to perform instead and proved she could by perfectly mimicking the poem Ruby was going to read, Ruby allowed her little understudy to take her place. Dorothy was a hit, and her mother was understandably quite pleased.

Dorothy and her older sister were soon in demand for performances at black churches throughout Cleveland. Dorothy later wrote, "Vivian said she wanted to play the piano, and she did learn to play, but piano never interested me. I wanted to dance and cavort and act all over the stage."[10] Ruby wrote dramatic routines and funny skits, drilled the girls in poetry memorization, and taught them how to sing and dance for an audience.

When Dorothy was around four-years-old, Ruby's church friend Geneva Williams, who was fleeing her own failed marriage to a minister,[11] moved in with Ruby and the girls. "Neva" was a gifted performer, vocalist, and teacher who had studied at Fisk University in her hometown of Nashville, Tennessee. The girls didn't understand it at the time, but Ruby and Neva soon became intimately involved. Biographer Donald Bogle later noted that "they had found in one another what no man could offer them."[12]

Ruby assumed the duties of breadwinning and budgeting, and Neva, whom the girls were instructed to call "Auntie Ma-Ma," took on the roles of homemaker and caregiver to the girls, nicknamed "Vivi" and "Dottie." Neva taught and coached the girls in singing, music, dancing, and acrobatics. They were not enrolled in school, so Neva also taught them math and reading. Neva was a strict authoritarian, and her disciplinary tactics frequently devolved into physical violence, especially against Dorothy. The little girls had no choice but to submit to the woman who had come into their home. Dorothy would write somewhat wistfully that "in nothing did she endear herself to me. I had a crying childhood."[13]

When Neva's grandmother died, Neva was needed back in Nashville with her family, leaving Ruby without someone to care for the children, so the two women decided that the girls would go with Neva, and Ruby would join them later. The decision may have also been swayed by Ruby's ongoing divorce and child custody proceedings with Cyril, who would never be able to find them if they headed to Tennessee. This separation from the only parent left in her life served to heighten Dorothy's already profound feelings of insecurity.[14]

---

[10] Dandridge and Conrad, 14.

[11] Bogle, 15-16.

[12] Ibid., 24.

[13] Dandridge and Conrad, 18-19.

[14] Bogle, 19.

Once settled in Tennessee, Neva resumed the girls' grueling training schedule and worked with her local contacts to secure arrangements for them to perform. They set out appearing in small venues in Tennessee on behalf of a black university. Later, after Ruby's arrival, they performed at schools and Baptist churches throughout the South for wages of their own. Dubbed the "Wonder Children," the act earned hundreds of dollars per performance. "Vivian and I became the best-dressed little girls in the country," Dorothy wrote.[15] Ruby and Neva also performed, as shows lasted up to three hours each. Since they were black in the South in the 1920s, the women taught the girls how to read "White" and "Colored" signs so they could successfully navigate the racial segregation. It was a monotonous, lonely, and exhausting lifestyle, but through it all, Dorothy's craving to perform intensified.

The Great Depression ended this tour around 1931, when Dorothy was near the age of eight-years-old. The family headed north in search of work and ended up in Chicago,[16] but work and food were scarce, to the extent that they relied on welfare. Nonetheless, Ruby was determined to build a better life and remained optimistic about her girls' talent. Two years earlier, a National Urban League publication had proclaimed, "It's the day of the dark star in Hollywood." Thus, Hollywood is where Ruby audaciously set her sights, and she eventually scraped, scrounged, and saved enough money to buy four bus tickets to Hollywood.

The first contact she met with in California told Ruby that the girls' skin wasn't dark enough for them to find work there. "He insisted that the studios wanted *Colored-looking* Colored people," Bogle wrote. This attempt at discouragement motivated Ruby.[17]

The family settled in Los Angeles' Watts neighborhood. By now, Vivian had grown into a vivacious, outgoing girl with a lively sense of humor, meaning that she took after her mother. Though their father was absent, Dorothy was very much like him, with a sensitive and friendly personality. She was also naturally attractive, and even at her tender age, she'd already proven herself a disciplined professional who was able to memorize lines, sing, dance, and perform acrobatics.[18]

For the first time, the girls were enrolled in public school, where some of Dorothy's playmates became lifelong friends. They also took lessons at a dance school while Ruby worked odd jobs and Neva conducted piano and voice lessons out of their home. Dance school classmate Etta Jones was also taking voice lessons from Neva, so she and the Dandridge girls became friends. They laughed and played together, and they danced and sang.

When Ruby heard how good they sounded together, she saw dollar signs. She immediately set

[15] Dandridge and Conrad, 23.
[16] Ibid., 32.
[17] Bogle, 35.
[18] Ibid., 51, 77.

to work grooming and refining them as "The Dandridge Sisters," a harmonious trio with an elegant, mature image beyond their young teenage years. They were beautiful, disciplined, and well-mannered.[19] The trio sang with a black youth choir for two years, then formed the quintet "The Five Rhythmatics," dancing, singing, and performing skits with two brothers. The quintet performed on weekends in and around southern California, and they worked on-and-off together for five years.[20] Meanwhile, Ruby worked and networked with the Works Progress Administration's theater program.

Lillian Randolph, Ernest Whitman, and Ruby Dandridge of the radio cast of *The Beulah Show*

[19] Ibid., 37-39.

[20] Ibid., 40.

The Dandridge Sisters

Back in Cleveland, Cyril still sought his wife and daughters, though their trail had gone cold to him in 1930. Finally, in the summer of 1933, on his lawyer's advice, Cyril filed a public petition for divorce from Ruby. When she didn't respond to newspaper advertisements seeking her, the divorce was granted on July 21.[21]

Sadly, Dorothy and Vivian's home life was no happier than it was when they were little girls. Though they were teenagers, Neva still beat them regularly and tightly bound their developing breasts with muslin cloth every day. "Now's the time to keep you from getting big as a cow," Neva declared. "The way you're growing out, big men will stare at you."[22] As before, Ruby deferred to Neva in such matters, which forced the girls to cope with the ongoing abuse in their own ways. Dorothy withdrew into herself and privately became moody and depressed.[23]

---

[21] Ibid., 44.
[22] Dandridge and Conrad, 41.

The Dandridge Sisters' first major break came in 1934 when they won an amateur talent contest on a Los Angeles radio show. They spent the 1935 Christmas season singing and dancing in a circus sideshow act in Hawaii, where Dorothy, at age 13, experienced her first taste of romance. She fell hard for a young island boy and shared her first kiss with him. The Hawaii trip also unexpectedly ended Dorothy's formal education when her Los Angeles school refused to apply work she completed at Hawaii schools toward her high school diploma.[24]

The girls began working with composer and arranger Phil Moore, and were held to a busy schedule of live performances, but Ruby felt compelled to seek out movie appearances for the girls as well. Through her connections, the trio was cast for a song-and-dance sequence in Paramount Pictures' *The Big Broadcast of 1936*, a musical revue that showcased radio and vaudeville stars. The 1936 edition featured Bing Crosby, George Burns, Gracie Allen, Ethel Merman, and tap-dancing sensations Fayard and Harold Nicholas, two young brothers who would go on to play a bigger role in Dorothy's life down the road.[25]

[23] Bogle, 53.
[24] Ibid., 42.
[25] Ibid., 58-59.

The Nicholas Brothers and Bob Hope

For the next several years, the Dandridge Sisters performed musical numbers for movies and rubbed elbows with some of the major stars of the day, including Clark Gable, the Marx Brothers, Ralph Bellamy, and Louis Armstrong. Still, the performers, studio executives, and film crews expressed and experienced different types and degrees of racial discrimination. "Once the cameras rolled, talent was respected. Once the cameras stopped, the Black performers were confronted with the familiar biases and prejudices," Bogle wrote.[26]

Armstrong introduced Ruby and the Dandridge Sisters to his manager, Joe Glaser, who agreed to represent them.[27] The introduction occurred while they all were working on a Warner Brothers musical comedy aptly titled *Going Places*, and Glaser soon made sure the Dandridge Sisters were going places themselves.

Glaser and Louis Armstrong

The Dandridge Sisters

Cigarette and reefer haze rises and shrouds the primitive decor of the broad, terraced Cotton Club in a wispy fog. Heavy carpet muffles the steady buzz of celebrity gossip and table talk. [28]

---

[26] Ibid., 47.

[27] Ibid., 48.

Prohibition ended five years ago, but seedy underworld types still lurk about. Sugar daddies linger over their drinks at the bar and fawn over the "tall, tan, and terrific"[29] chorus girls as they prance and sashay about in sensual, revealing costumes of outlandishly oversized feathers and not much else. The crowd applauses thunderously as the orchestra swings into a sultry introduction. Cab Calloway saunters and sways about the stage and enthusiastically beckons participation in a rhythmic call-and-response refrain that frenetically crescendos to a climactic explosion of nonsensical syncopated syllables. The crowd goes wild.

Calloway

Situated just off Broadway in Midtown Manhattan, the Cotton Club was the place for elegant, sophisticated white movers and shakers to watch the nation's top black entertainers. Manager Joe Glaser was so impressed with The Dandridge Sisters that this was his choice for an extended booking for them. He recruited Phil Moore to write fresh arrangements. Ruby could not leave her

---

28 Dandridge and Conrad, 48.

29 Bogle, 55.

job in Los Angeles, so the girls headed east with Neva in late summer 1938. Dorothy was 15 when Neva and the girls settled into a Harlem apartment in the same building as the Peters Sisters, another young trio of singers with backgrounds and experiences similar to the Dandridge Sisters. The six girls became fast friends and spent most of their free time exploring the Big Apple together.[30]

The Peters Sisters

Dorothy, Vivian, and Etta were chiefly occupied with singing and dancing rehearsals, gown fittings, and other meetings in preparation for their impending debut at the legendary venue,

---

[30] Ibid., 54.

which had also hosted Duke Ellington, Lena Horne, Cab Calloway, and the aforementioned Nicholas Brothers. [31] By the time the tapdancing brothers' paths crossed with the Dandridge Sisters at the Cotton Club in 1938, Fayard and Harold Nicholas were superstars who had been performing professionally at nightclubs, in Hollywood movies, and on Broadway for years. Aptly nicknamed "The Little Princes of Harlem,"[32] the Nicholas Brothers were rich, sophisticated, and accustomed to all the trimmings and trappings of stardom.

The moment younger brother Harold saw Dorothy at the Cotton Club, he was smitten. Her wholesome naiveté and sweet innocence were quite the contrast to his seductive charm and wild reputation, but she was flattered by his attention and they quickly became friends.[33] Of course, Harold was not the only male lavishing attention on Dorothy as she grew up, because she was stunningly beautiful. Bogle explained, "But all those hot and horny fellows at the Cotton Club knew that no matter how much they might salivate or how strong they might come on, she was not one of those easy overnight conquests. In fact, not a conquest at all. If a fellow enjoyed the chase, then Dottie was perfect because a chase was all a guy would get."

Dorothy and Harold's courtship consisted of the two Nicholas Brothers visiting the three Dandridge Sisters at their Harlem apartment, or the sisters visiting the Nicholas family's home nearby.[34] "It was as corny as the stalks in Iowa," Dorothy wrote. "It was a puritanical, idyllic relationship…replete with talk-talk, hot dogs, movies, chitlins, boxes of candy, long walks, hand-holding, flowers."[35] Neva hovered nearby through it all to keep hormones at bay, obsess over the girls' appearances, and satisfy her paranoia over preserving their virginity.[36]

The chaste young girls seemed an unusual choice for the sex-saturated nightclub scene, but the addition of their swift choral embellishments to the Cab Calloway-headlined blues show was hailed by critics as a success. Glowing reviews made newspaper headlines from coast to coast, and one of those reviews attracted the attention of Cyril Dandridge, Dorothy's and Vivian's estranged father, who still lived in Cleveland. [37] Cyril spoke to the girls on the telephone and immediately boarded a bus to New York to meet them. The reunion was awkward, as Ruby and Neva had been telling the girls for years that their father had either deserted them or died, and the visit was cut short when Dorothy left with Harold for a previously planned date. She later said she didn't care if she never saw him again. "All I could think of was, If I had turned out to be a criminal, if I had been in jail, would he have hurried to New York to see me?"[38]

---

[31] Ibid., 55.

[32] "The Nicholas Brothers: We Sing and We Dance." An A&E Biographic Production, 1992. Accessed January 15, 2020.

[33] Bogle, 61.

[34] Ibid., 62.

[35] Dandridge and Conrad, 44.

[36] Bogle, 56-57, 68.

[37] Ibid., 65-66.

[38] Dandridge and Conrad, 50-51.

The Dandridge Sisters' Cotton Club engagement lasted two seasons. The second season, they also performed at the Strand Theater just across the street. "Oh, it was just a mess but we loved it," Etta Jones later said. Toward the end of 1938, the Nicholas Brothers left for a South American tour, imposing a hiatus on Harold and Dorothy's budding romance. Around the same time, Joe Glaser set his sights on the United Kingdom, and The Dandridge Sisters' tour began in London on June 19, 1939. Dorothy was 17.

The girls again lodged near the Peters Sisters, who were also performing in London, and when the six girls again set off exploring together, they noticed far less racism than back home.[39] The trio performed around England, Ireland, and Scotland as clouds of war descended on Europe. World War II started in September 1939 as Nazi Germany began an invasion of their invasions and occupations of neighboring countries earlier that spring.

Clouds were also descending on Neva and Dorothy's relationship, as Neva's physical and emotional abuse intensified. After one of the girls' friends claimed Dorothy was pregnant, Neva snapped and flew into a frenzy. She accused Dorothy of sexual promiscuity, forced the terrified teen down on her bed, and tore off all of her clothes. Dorothy vividly described what happened: "She was trying to find out whether I was a virgin…she put her fingers inside…in spite of my resistance." This sexual violation awakened a spirit of resistance in Dorothy, and she finally fought back against Neva. "I had never struck her before, nor anyone, but it felt good," Dorothy wrote. "I walloped her hard…I clawed and scratched and punched…I had her against the wall and I pummeled and pummeled." After her fury waned, Dorothy fled and hid. "Inside, my embarrassment hurt…it seemed as if I could still feel her fingers there…That hurt worse than all her pounding."[40] This beating and sexual assault marked the last time Neva ever laid hands on Dorothy, but the effects would haunt Dorothy for the rest of her life.

When Great Britain and France declared war on Germany after its invasion of Poland on September 1, 1939, Neva and The Dandridge Sisters cut their tour short and quickly sailed home, but the girls had no break upon their arrival back in the United States. They returned to the Cotton Club for three performances a night, appeared in the short run of the Broadway musical *Swingin' the Dream*, and headed out on the road to perform in Washington, D.C, and Chicago. Arrangements had begun for a South American tour of their own, but those plans were scrapped when Neva needed to return to Los Angeles and took the girls with her. By then, Harold and Fayard Nicholas had landed there too, this time to work on a series of films under their groundbreaking and lucrative five-year contract with 20th Century Fox.[41]

Dorothy and Harold resumed their courtship, but they were again interrupted by show business. The Dandridge Sisters joined the national tour of Jimmie Lunceford and His Orchestra, a

---

[39] Bogle, 66-67.
[40] Dandridge and Conrad, 54-56; Bogle, 70-71.
[41] Bogle, 73-74.

disciplined, classy swing-era big band whose impeccable style and snazzy showmanship the girls complemented perfectly. The trio toured with Lunceford for a year and a half, and they even performed on four records with the outfit. One of them, "Red Wagon,"[42] became a hit.[43]

Lunceford

By the end of the tour, Dorothy was 18 and eager to launch a solo career. Etta Jones got married, which Dorothy interpreted as the end of The Dandridge Sisters, but Etta had planned to remain with the trio. Etta later said, "Dorothy's aspirations broke up the Dandridge Sisters…she cut us loose."

Dorothy auditioned for and landed a role in the play *Meet the People,* a satirical sketch musical. She also worked for several low-budget and all-black film production companies and performed one-nighters up and down the West Coast. In 1941, Harold and Fayard convinced Fox producers that adding Dorothy to their performance in the song "Chattanooga Choo Choo"[44] in

---

[42] "Red Wagon," youtube.com, accessed January 17, 2020.

[43] Bogle, 76.

the movie *Sun Valley Serenade* would infuse the number with sex appeal and romance, and they were right. Actress and dancer Debbie Allen recalled, "Dorothy Dandridge with the Nicholas Brothers was just like puttin' butter on a hot biscuit, child!"[45] Larger roles in stage musicals and films soon followed, along with appearances in "Soundies," which were short musical films that played on Panoram jukebox-like consoles equipped with screens.[46] Vivian and Ruby also landed film and voice work.[47] For the most part, however, Hollywood in the early 1940s wasn't quite ready to cast black actors and actresses in anything other than stereotypical roles, such as servants, and Dorothy already appeared far too sophisticated for such parts.[48]

Dorothy and Harold continued seeing each other when proximity and schedules allowed. In January 1942, Fayard Nicholas married Geri Pate, a long-time fan who finally introduced herself to him a month earlier. That June, Vivian got married. Finally, Harold and Dorothy set a wedding date of September 6, 1942. The groom and bride were 21 and 19 when they were married, and they purchased an enchanting little cottage near Harold's mother's house, happily shopping and redecorating it to make it a comfortable, cozy home. "It was a beautiful little house," Fayard said. "It was just made for them."[49]

Unfortunately, life was not as idyllic as it appeared. Starting on their wedding night, skeletons from both of their closets immediately began destroying the marriage. "I was inexperienced, fearful enough to be cold," Dorothy later wrote of their wedding night. "I didn't know what to do. Harold had much experience with girls, so whatever he expected he didn't get. I tried not to show it, but everything in my background contributed to making me feel that this normal event was a violation." Within days, Dorothy suspected that Harold was seeing a chorus girl.[50] Despite Dorothy's protestations, Harold spent less and less time at home. Then the couple was in a car accident, and Dorothy was hospitalized with back injuries. Harold did not visit her, but Fayard's wife Geri did, and the two women became faithful confidants and lifelong friends. Geri was able to break through Dorothy's seemingly haughty, self-preserving exterior and see her for the honest, generous spirit she truly was.[51]

In early 1943, Harold and Fayard filmed the greatest tap-dance routine not only of their own career, but arguably in film history: the finale of the movie *Stormy Weather*.[52] The scene was shot hastily because Fayard had been drafted into the U.S. Army. Harold also received notice,

---

[44] "Chattanooga Choo Choo," youtube.com, accessed January 17, 2020.

[45] The Nicholas Brothers: We Sing and We Dance.

[46] "1939 Mills Panoram." Torrence Collection, on youtube.com, accessed January 20, 2020. Many of Dorothy's Soundies can easily be found on youtube.com.

[47] Bogle, 102.

[48] Ibid., 97.

[49] Ibid., 105.

[50] Dandridge and Conrad, 61-62.

[51] Bogle, 106-110.

[52] "Jumpin' Jive," twistedsifter.com, Feb. 8, 2018. Accessed January 20, 2020.

but when he reported for his physical, he was marked exempt, because at 5'2" tall, Harold was an inch short of the minimal height requirement.[53]

In March, Dorothy discovered that she was pregnant. She hoped that impending parenthood would settle Harold down and draw him back home, but he continued with his own pursuits. When Dorothy went into labor on September 1, 1943, Harold drove her to Fayard and Geri's house. When he left with a friend, he left the car with the women, but he forgot to leave the keys. Dorothy's contractions intensified, but she refused to go to the hospital without Harold. Finally, after her water broke, Geri and a neighbor convinced Dorothy she had to go. The delivery was difficult, and doctors used forceps to deliver the baby. Dorothy's baby girl was born just before 3:00 a.m. on September 2. Harold arrived an hour later.[54]

The couple named their daughter Harolyn Suzanne Nicholas, after her father, and she looked like him. Laughter, smiles, and hugs filled their home as the couple doted on their baby, whom they called "Lynn." Ruby, Neva, and Harold's mother all contributed heartily to the spoiling of their adorable granddaughter. Fayard's military commitment ended after 13 months, and he and Geri soon had a baby son named Tony.

The young families settled into a new routine filled with parenting, homemaking, socializing, and entertaining. The Nicholas brothers' status kept the two couples in the heady company of black Hollywood's elite, and Fayard and Harold continued performing.[55] Dorothy and Geri periodically went along on their husbands' tours, leaving the babies in their capable nannies' care. As the babies grew, it became easier for Dorothy and Geri to take them along on road trips.

Lynn and Tony learned to walk, and Tony learned to talk, but Lynn did not. Lynn had frequent temper tantrums, and it soon seemed that Lynn did not recognize familiar people, not even her own mother. Dorothy tried to tell Harold that she thought something was wrong with their daughter, but he wouldn't listen.[56] Harold and Dorothy blamed themselves for Lynn's condition, but they coped differently. Harold withdrew from his family, while Dorothy was compelled by her frustrations to obtain a diagnosis. Geri accompanied Dorothy on her rounds with Lynn to pediatricians, specialists, psychoanalysts, and therapists.

When Dorothy finally received honest medical feedback about Lynn, it was grim; Lynn's development had been impaired by a lack of blood or oxygen flow to the speech and abstract thinking centers of her brain.[57] Lynn's mental capacity would never advance beyond that of a six-year-old child. One doctor even advised Dorothy, "The best thing for you to do is to get rid

---

[53] Constance Valis-Hill. *Brotherhood in Rhythm: The Jazz Tap Dancing of the Nicholas Brothers* (New York: Cooper Square Press, 2002), 215.

[54] Bogle, 112.

[55] Ibid., 114-115.

[56] Dandridge and Conrad, 69.

[57] Dandridge and Conrad, 73.

of her. Give her up and have another baby."[58]

The strain of her floundering marriage on top of caring for Lynn and seeking answers about her development took a heavy toll on Dorothy, and she began seeing a psychiatrist. She wrote that "the only year or two of happiness in my life was in the time before I discovered how hopeless Lynn was."[59] Furthermore, as Lynn grew older, she grew stronger and more difficult to control. Dorothy's psychiatrist advised her she needed a break, and that she should find a permanent alternative caregiver for Lynn. She tried, but to no avail, and in desperation she finally turned Lynn over to Ruby and Neva. The grandmothers were happy to care for Lynn, but only if they were paid $50 a week.[60]

Outwardly, Dorothy shifted her focus back onto herself. She went to parties with Geri, and the friends worked on fundraisers for social, political, and civil rights causes. She became one of the first black students at the Actors Laboratory, a progressive dramatic acting school, where Marilyn Monroe was one of her classmates.[61] Harold and Fayard launched an extensive multi-year tour through Europe, including stops in England, France, Switzerland, Sweden, and Portugal. Dorothy and Geri periodically joined them in the glamorous realm of the rich, titled elite to attend posh parties, elegant luncheons, sophisticated receptions, and fashionable performances.[62] Upon their return from one of those overseas trips, Dorothy discovered that Ruby and Neva were paying Helen Calhoun, a specialized caregiver, $50 a month to watch Lynn and pocketing the extra $150. Dorothy transferred Lynn to Calhoun's care.[63]

---

[58] Ibid., 75-76.
[59] Ibid., 80.
[60] Bogle, 129-133
[61] Ibid., 152-153.
[62] Ibid., 136.
[63] Dandridge and Conrad, 78.

Marilyn Monroe

Harold and Fayard soon dropped all pretenses and stopped hiding their philandering. This openness humiliated their wives even more deeply than the infidelity. Dorothy landed in hospitals twice after overdosing on sleeping pills, but both times she insisted she simply couldn't sleep.[64]

Making matters worse, Harold stopped sending Dorothy money, making it difficult for her to cover her bills. He also stopped accepting her calls and did not respond to her messages. Finally, Dorothy heard Harold signed a long-term contract in Italy. She recounted feeling like "it was clear to me he was dismissing me. I was being pushed out, dropped, abandoned. Like a gentleman, Harold allowed me to get the divorce."[65]

After five years of marriage, Dorothy was on her own. She was still just 26.

Breaking New Ground

"You can't do without friends in this world." - Dorothy Dandridge[66]

With no funds and no spousal support, Dorothy needed to rely on herself, and not surprisingly,

---

[64] Ibid., 143.
[65] Dandridge and Conrad, 80-81.
[66] Dandridge and Conrad, 104.

she turned to entertainment. After a chance encounter with Phil Moore, Dorothy dropped his name to Charlie Morrison, the owner of Sunset Boulevard's hip and happening, tropical-themed Mocambo nightclub, in hopes of landing a gig there, but Morrison didn't think she was ready for his club yet.

Phil Moore (foreground)

Dorothy's path had last crossed Moore's when he was an arranger for The Dandridge Sisters' gig at The Cotton Club. Since then, Moore had become the first black musician hired by a Hollywood studio. Keeping Dorothy's cinematic aspirations in mind, the pair began working on her nightclub act as Moore took Dorothy under his wing. He wrote arrangements for her and rehearsed with her. He advised her on her wardrobe, hairstyles, and makeup. He confronted her anxieties and directed her ambitions. He fell in love with her and tenderly called her his "Dottie Mae." She returned his affection, but she could not find it in herself to tell him she loved him back. "I had been too hurt by Harold to let myself go that way with anyone, as yet," she wrote.[67]

Dorothy performed a string of one-nighters at nightclubs around Los Angeles, with mixed results. She had panic attacks after several appearances, leading her to seek therapy, but she soldiered on. Finally, when Moore heard that the singer for Desi Arnaz's band, which was performing at the Mocambo, had fallen ill and was unable to perform, Moore convinced Morrison to let Dorothy substitute. The gig was a success and resulted in longer bookings not only in and around Los Angeles, but also in Lake Tahoe, New York, and Las Vegas. Though the stages in Sin City welcomed black performers, Las Vegas was segregated by bigoted racial codes. Black stars were not allowed to lodge in the chic new hotels on the Strip, even if they were performing there, and they were prohibited from entering dining rooms and casinos.[68]

Despite the rampant racism, Dorothy was dazzling, and the media started to notice. Dorothy hired a publicist to further increase press coverage, and she was soon offered supporting roles in two low-budget movies in October 1950. In the melodrama *The Harlem Globetrotters*, Dorothy played the love interest of Bill Brown, who starred as himself in the movie, and in *Tarzan's Peril*, Dorothy played the young queen of an African village who is rescued from a kidnapper by Tarzan, played by a white actor. These portrayals garnered attention from magazines, including *Variety*, *Jet*, and *Ebony*, the last of which crowned Dorothy "Hollywood's New Glamour Queen."[69]

Early in 1951, Jim Dolan, the owner of Café Gala, was looking for new performers for his venue and thought Moore would be a good fit. Café Gala was an intimate, elegant little club two blocks west yet seemingly a world away from the flamboyant Mocambo on Sunset. Once a private residence, Café Gala was patronized exclusively by white socialites and movie stars. Moore convinced Dolan to instead consider Dorothy for the gig, which she landed because Moore agreed to be her accompanist. Dorothy was intimidated at the prospect of performing for Hollywood's upper crust, as flopping in front of that crowd could end her fledgling movie career. On her opening night, she was so nervous she could barely sing, but as her set went on, Moore helped her relax and regain her composure. Within a few nights, she was back on top of her game.[70] *Los Angeles Mirror* entertainment editor Dick Williams was enthralled. He gushed, "The satiny, sexy songstress has that starlight aura. She has beauty, an infectious good humor, sexy delivery and an extremely clever style. This is Dorothy Dandridge, the most exciting new sepia singer I've spotted."[71]

---

[67] Ibid., 84.
[68] Bogle, 170-171.
[69] Ibid., 181-185.
[70] Ibid., 189-191.
[71] Mills, 92-93.

Buzz about the new sensation at Café Gala traveled fast, so it didn't take long to reach Morrison up Sunset Boulevard. He now thought she was ready for the Mocambo. "More than simply being a place to see and be seen, the Mocambo was also a pleasure palace of fun, energy, intrigue, adventure, and the entertainment matched the sophistication of the clientele," biographer Bogle later wrote.[72] Dorothy took ballet and modern dance lessons to prepare for the important gig and also worked with a vocal coach. She opened at the Mocambo on May 7, 1951, and her performance quickly set Hollywood's dignitaries all abuzz. Her next engagement, at London's elegant Café de Paris, was just as fabulous. Reviews described how she cast a captivating spell the moment she gracefully drifted down the club's opulent rococo staircase.

Moore was thrilled by Dorothy's mounting success, but he was growing jealous of the increasing adoration that was being lavished on her, and Dorothy was growing weary of the increasingly possessive and controlling manner with which Moore treated her. Earlier that spring, Moore had introduced Dorothy to his manager, Earl Mills. When she sang for Mills at a private party, he was struck by her beauty and impressed by her performance. "She poured herself into the melody and caressed the words," Mills noted. He firmly believed in her talent and told her he could help her career.[73] After Dorothy and Moore had a public falling out at a club in London, they returned home barely speaking to each other. In November, talent agent Berle Adams invited Dorothy to appear on Dean Martin and Jerry Lewis' television variety show, but Moore convinced her she wasn't ready for national exposure. Adams disagreed, and after he had a heated argument with Moore, Dorothy performed on the show.[74] Later that month, Dorothy and Moore formally agreed to part ways, and Mills officially became her manager. Mills soon hired accompanist Morty Jacobs to work with Dorothy.[75]

By December, Dorothy and Moore were working together again, this time with no romantic strings attached. Dorothy was booked to sing at Manhattan's La Vie en Rose nightclub, and she needed Moore's direction and calming. Despite her mounting insecurities over performing for a live audience, she dazzled the opening night crowd. *Time* magazine described how Dorothy, in a slinky gold gown, "came wriggling out of the wings like a caterpillar on a hot rock."[76] Her two-week engagement was extended to 14 weeks, with three shows on some nights. She hit her stride, and people couldn't get enough of the bombshell. *Look*, *Ebony*, *Theatre Arts*, and *Our World* magazines featured her in photos and articles, and she appeared on Ed Sullivan's television show, Jackie Gleason's show, and Steve Allen's show.

The publicity led to plans for a nationwide tour, which began in May 1952 and included stops in St. Louis, Pittsburgh, Lake Tahoe, and Dorothy's hometown of Cleveland. Moore hired pianist

---

[72] Bogle, 193-194.

[73] Mills, 90.

[74] Dorothy Dandridge on *The Colgate Comedy Hour*, November 4, 1951. youtube.com, accessed January 28, 2020.

[75] Bogle, 194, 199-204.

[76] Ibid., 208.

Nick Perito as director, accompanist, and orchestral conductor for the tour.

Times were changing, but despite her rising fame, Dorothy continued to experience all kinds of racist treatment. The Chase Hotel in St. Louis bent its rules and permitted her to stay there, but management instructed her to stay out of the establishment's public areas and away from guests. Perito, who was white, was appalled by such bigotry, and he insisted on escorting Dorothy through the Chase's lobby and invited her to dine with him in its café.[77] Perito complained, "Dorothy was constantly reminded that she was *different*.... She felt that she didn't belong anywhere. She was not really accepted by her own race, because they felt her behavioral patterns were too white and, on the other hand, the whites regarded her as a Negro—therefore, she was subject to all of their racial discrimination—except when she was performing on stage. This would cause her a lot of emotional stress, pain, and sorrow in years to come."[78]

Ruby joined Dorothy in Cleveland, where her father again tried to reconnect with her. Dorothy initially agreed to attend church with Cyril, but she later backed out on him via a telegram. "I don't know this man," she told a friend at the time.[79]

In the years after Dorothy's romance with Moore soured, Dorothy was involved in a string of serious but brief romances. She kept company with singer and actor Harry Belafonte, then a young and rising star, but he ended the relationship when he felt threatened by her success.[80] Then came Hardie Albright, a charming, boyish white actor who ended things with Dorothy when both realized she couldn't possibly earn enough money to satiate his worldly desires.[81] Later came Peter Lawford, the gallant and debonair British socialite and Rat Pack actor whom Dorothy introduced to Jim Crow and chitterlings. Lawford would not pop the one question Dorothy most wanted to hear from him.[82] Still later, she fantasized about a picture-perfect Christmas with her Austrian costar Curt Jurgens at his villa in Vienna, but he was there with his mistress and their new baby.[83] "Finding a man who wanted to go to bed was the easiest thing in the world," Dorothy wrote. "Finding a serious man was one of the most difficult."[84]

---

[77] Ibid., 213.

[78] Nick Perito, *I Just Happened to be There: Making Music with the Stars*, 2004 (Bloomington, Indiana: Xlibris Corporation), 102.

[79] Bogle, 215.

[80] Dandridge and Conrad, 92.

[81] Ibid., 96-100.

[82] Ibid., 110-114.

[83] Bogle, 391, 402.

[84] Dandridge and Conrad, 95.

Belafonte with Julie Andrews

Carmen Jones

"When you reach a certain position, people accept you more, and there are places where you are acclaimed as a performer, yet you know the doors would be shut if you walked in as plain Mrs. Sally Smith." - Dorothy Dandridge[85]

During her 1952 tour, Dorothy took a detour to New York to discuss her consideration for the lead role in the low-budget MGM film *Bright Road*, but she also had a less pleasant matter to address. The United States was consumed by the Red Scare, the Cold War-era hunt for Communists, and Hollywood was eager to assure audiences that its productions were free from Soviet influence. Nobody was immune to the poison pen of Hedda Hopper, the libelous Hollywood gossip columnist whose red-tinged accusations caught the attention of paranoid government investigators and landed subjects on industry blacklists. Hopper cast suspicion on Dorothy based on Dorothy's past association with Actor's Laboratory and actor Paul Robeson,

---

[85] Bogle, 309.

both of which were deemed Communist by private patriotic groups. Dorothy felt compelled to answer Hopper's accusations and clear her name, so she drafted a written statement to that effect.[86]

Dorothy began to work on *Bright Road* in Hollywood in August 1952. Set in Alabama, the film had a nearly all-black cast. Dorothy played an idealistic young schoolteacher, and New York folk singer Harry Belafonte, in his first film role, played the school principal.[87] Dorothy prepared carefully and worked diligently for her performance, but nonetheless drew painful comparisons between her on-set students and her daughter Lynn. "When I walked on the set and saw the colored children—about the same age as Lynn—when I saw how happy and smiling they were, I started crying and had to leave the set," Dorothy explained.[88] By the time filming on *Bright Road* wrapped, Dorothy was romantically involved with director Gerald Mayer, but when on set Dorothy characteristically kept to herself. She and Mayer drifted apart after about a year.[89]

Media accolades continued to flow when Dorothy went back on the road. Her glamorous gown collection was insured for $250,000, and she traveled with an assistant to keep that wardrobe and other more mundane details in order. Her days were filled with appearances, interviews, and photoshoots, as well as fundraisers for advocacy groups for handicapped children. Upon *Bright Road*'s release in April 1953, Dorothy's performance earned positive reviews and a cover feature in *Ebony* magazine.[90]

Still, even as her status was skyrocketing, Dorothy remained the target of discrimination. As the Chase Hotel in St. Louis had done earlier, the Last Frontier on the Las Vegas Strip loosened its racist policy and rented Dorothy a room, but she was ordered to stay out of the swimming pool. When she objected to this restriction, management drained the pool.[91]

That summer, Dorothy embarked on a tour of Brazil with Morty Jacobs as her accompanist. She was refreshed by the racial tolerance and the subsequent freedom she experienced. She also experienced no shortage of amorous attention from Latin Lotharios. She was swept off her feet by an impossibly wealthy, dashing young businessman who wooed her with his fleet of limousines, his familiarity with the vibrant and dramatic beauty of Rio de Janeiro, and his collection of cosmopolitan, beachfront, and mountainside estates, but Dorothy was devastated to discover he wanted her to be his mistress.[92] Perched on her hotel window ledge, she called Jacobs' room and told him, "I'm not afraid to die, but I feel terrible because I want to die."[93] Jacobs summoned a Brazilian doctor, and the doctor gave her an opioid shot to clear her head.[94]

---

[86] Ibid., 217-222.

[87] Ibid., 225.

[88] Dandridge and Conrad, 128.

[89] Bogle, 234.

[90] Ibid., 234.

[91] Ibid., 238-239.

[92] Dandridge and Conrad, 150.

[93] Bogle, 249-250

After her tour of Brazil, Dorothy returned home to headline at the Mocambo nightclub, a smashing success that marked her arrival at the pinnacle of the nation's nightclub culture. Though reviewers used adjectives like "SEXsation" to describe her, Dorothy always aimed to appear dignified and elegant. She was not comfortable being described and depicted as sexy.[95]

Regardless of her efforts, Dorothy's next role would cement her status as a sex symbol. In December 1953, Hollywood magnate Otto Preminger signed with 20th Century Fox to direct and produce the film *Carmen Jones*, a musical with an all-black cast. The film would be based on the popular 1943 Broadway play by Oscar Hammerstein II, which in turn was based on the 1875 French opera *Carmen* by Georges Bizet.[96] Preminger cast Harry Belafonte for the male lead, as well as Pearl Bailey and Diahann Carroll for supporting roles. He still needed actresses to play the prim and proper girl-next-door, Cindy Lou, and also the title character, Carmen, a sensuous, duplicitous girl. Dorothy wanted to be Carmen. Preminger agreed to meet with Dorothy, who arrived for the interview in her naturally ladylike manner, wearing a flared blue dress with a modest Peter Pan collar, her hair pulled back in a ponytail.

"Now, Miss Dandridge, what makes you think that you can do Carmen?" Preminger asked condescendingly.

"Well, Mr. Preminger, what makes you think I can't?"

Ultimately, he agreed to let Dorothy read for him as Cindy Lou, but Dorothy wanted to be Carmen, and Preminger's patronization only strengthened Dorothy's resolve. She was determined, and she was angry. That night, under the direction of her mother and her sister, Dorothy practiced strutting and swishing and swinging her hips. She bought a tousled wig, a slinky slit skirt, and a revealing off-the-shoulder blouse. She arrived fashionably late for her appointment with Preminger and sidled seductively through his doorway. "My God!" Preminger exclaimed. "It's Carmen!" With that, Dorothy landed the role.

Dorothy immediately began hearing envious and resentful feedback from the black community over Preminger's choice. Overwhelmed by self-doubt, she nearly refused the role. Preminger had earned his reputation as an impartially harsh and demanding taskmaster on set, but he gently persuaded her to ignore the naysayers, and by the time production work began, though Preminger was still married to his second wife, he and Dorothy were romantically involved.[97] He was 48 and she was 31.

---

94 Dandridge and Conrad, 154.
95 Bogle, 256.
96 Ibid., 264.
97 Ibid., 271-273.

Preminger (seated)

Despite the fact that Dorothy and Belafonte were professional singers, their characters' vocal tracks were recorded by opera singers. Pearl Bailey and Olga James, a recent Julliard School of Music graduate who was cast as Cindy Lou, did their own singing. Dorothy's Carmen was voiced by young mezzo-soprano Marilyn Horne, who later became a world-renowned opera superstar. The women spent hours studying each other's movements and mannerisms to achieve a seamless and believable dub, but for the most part, as usual, Dorothy kept her distance from fellow cast members.[98]

Dorothy's Carmen was independent and defiant, and much the way she succeeded in her nightclub performances, she expertly added depth and emotion to her songs by the way she moved and used her hands. By the time filming wrapped, Preminger believed Dorothy deserved consideration equal to what then-ascending superstars Marilyn Monroe and Elizabeth Taylor were receiving. He made it his personal mission to see that Dorothy, too, would rise to the top.[99]

The months leading up to the *Carmen Jones* premiere were a whirlwind of publicity. Dorothy was featured as the "Lady Fair" pinup for the June 1954 issue of *Esquire* and became the first

---

[98] Ibid., 276-278.
[99] Ibid., 288-289.

black woman featured on the cover of *Life* magazine.[100] Dressed as Carmen, Dorothy appeared on the issue dated November 1, 1954. So momentous was the occasion that when the issue hit stands several days earlier, a *Movietone News* crew shot a newsreel video clip of her, Preminger, and a *Life* magazine executive beaming over the magazine. [101]

Carmen Jones premiered at the Rivoli Theatre on Broadway in New York City on October 28. Glitterati from all walks of entertainment life turned out, including Dorothy and the movie cast, Preminger and Hammerstein, Count Basie, Sammy Davis, Jr., and Lena Horne. At the end of the movie, the audience gave a standing ovation.[102] Afterward, Dorothy was a guest on *The Tonight Show* with Steve Allen.

New York critics were dazzled by the movie, calling Dorothy "seductive," "a bewitcher," and "an incandescent Carmen." After *Carmen Jones'* Hollywood opening a few days later, West Coast critics followed suit. Her friend Geri, then writing for *The California Eagle*, opined that "Carmen is a tramp, but with such dignity you have to respect her right to the end." Even gossip columnist Hedda Hopper offered a glowing review: "Hope you won't repeat my experience when you see *Carmen Jones*. I got so excited I burned a big hole in the front of my dress. Yes the film is that hot."[103] Critics were not alone in their praise, as *Carmen Jones* became a hit at the box office as well.[104]

Academy Award buzz began almost immediately, and honors and accolades kept pouring in. In December, Dorothy served on the sponsorship committee for the National Urban League's glamorous annual Winter Ball. In January 1955, she was featured as one of *Ebony* magazine's "Five Most Beautiful Negro Women in the World," along with Lena Horne, Joyce Bryant, Hilda Simms, and Eartha Kitt.[105] On February 12, The Academy of Motion Picture Arts and Sciences announced its nominations for the 1954 Academy Awards. Best Actress nominees were Judy Garland for *A Star Is Born*, Audrey Hepburn for *Sabrina*, Grace Kelly for *The Country Girl*, Jane Wyman for *Magnificent Obsession*, and Dorothy Dandridge for *Carmen Jones*. Dorothy had just become the first black woman ever to be nominated for an Academy Award for Best Actress.[106]

Dorothy was on tour in Denver when she heard the news. Delighted, she immediately called Ruby and then Vivian to tell them. When they finished screaming, Dorothy invited Vivian to attend the ceremony with her. Later, Dorothy celebrated the nomination at a party with excited and optimistic friends. Preminger, however, was doubtful. "The time is not ripe," he predicted.

[100] Mills, 91. Jackie Robinson appeared on the May 8, 1950 cover.

[101] Bogle, 302.

[102] Mills, 159.

[103] Bogle, 304.

[104] Mills, 159.

[105] Bogle, 311-313.

[106] Two black actress had previously been nominated for an Academy Award for Best *Supporting* Actress—Hattie McDaniel, who won the award for *Gone with the Wind* in 1940, and Ethel Waters, nominated for *Pinky* in 1950.

Three days after the nomination, Dorothy signed a lucrative three-picture, non-exclusive contract with 20th Century Fox. She also landed a seven-week booking to begin in April in the Empire Room at the luxurious Waldorf Astoria Hotel on Park Avenue in New York. She would be the first black performer to appear at the landmark high-society venue. Then she was off to engagements at the Last Frontier in Las Vegas and the Fontainebleau in Miami, where she delighted critics and audiences alike. All the excitement was causing frequent insomnia, so Dorothy often took sleeping pills. She also began taking a tranquilizer to quell her anxiety.[107]

On March 30, Dorothy and Vivian rode in a limousine to the NBC Century Theater on Broadway in New York for the Academy Awards ceremony. The glitz and glamour lived up to all their childhood dreams. Dorothy proudly became the first black presenter of an Academy Award when she announced Gene Milford as the Best Film Editing winner for *On the Waterfront*. Later, William Holden took the podium to present the Best Actress award, which went to Grace Kelly for *The Country Girl*.[108]

Preminger had been right, but Dorothy had no time to wallow. She was scheduled to open the Empire Room on April 11. She was overcome by nerves and didn't know what to expect from a literal Fifth and Park Avenue audience, but beginning opening night, she held it under her spell. New York was enraptured,[109] and soon she seemed to have the whole world on a string. Wherever *Carmen Jones* was shown, Dorothy gained new fans, from London, West Germany, and Scandinavia to Latin America, Singapore, South Africa, and even France's Cannes Film Festival.[110] It seemed she could do no wrong.

The End

"In the last analysis what this society denied me was what it denies most women of color, perhaps all: simple respectability. If my story means anything, it means that the white millions still have to grant that simple and costless right to black women." - Dorothy Dandridge[111]

Though Dorothy appeared to have everything, she did not have the one thing she wanted most. She was hopeful for a happily ever after with Preminger, and she encouraged by the social airs their relationship assumed when they attended the 1955 Cannes Film Festival in Nice, France together. For six enchanting days, Preminger lavished Dorothy with attention, jewelry, and gifts, and the pair openly appeared together in public.[112] However, once they came back home, things returned to their clandestine version of normal, and Dorothy returned to film work. She was slated to play the supporting character Tuptim, a young concubine, in the upcoming musical *The*

[107] Bogle, 322-323, 341.
[108] Best Actress presentation at the 1955 Academy Awards, youtube.com. Accessed January 28, 2020.
[109] Bogle, 327.
[110] Ibid., 329-331.
[111] Dandridge and Conrad, 228.
[112] Bogle, 332.

King and I, but Dorothy felt the character was little more than a slave, a demeaning role to play. Preminger, certain that Dorothy deserved a leading role, agreed. After months of haggling with 20th Century Fox, Dorothy refused to play the role. In September, the studio recast Rita Moreno as Tuptim. The film went on to become a huge success, and Preminger's misguidance added strain to their increasingly tumultuous affair.

This setback was not the sole stressor in Dorothy's life. In August, her friend and longtime accompanist Nick Perito retired from road performing. Around the same time, Dorothy's sister Vivian, tired of vying with Dorothy for her mother's attention, permanently left the country and cut off all contact with her family.[113]

In November, Dorothy began an engagement at the Riviera Hotel in Las Vegas. The maître d'hôtel, Jack Denison, was known around town as a crafty manipulator and a womanizer, and he wanted very much to meet her. Denison arranged to have Dorothy's meals delivered to her room, and sent her flowers after every performance.[114] "Ordinarily I would have ignored this attention," Dorothy later wrote. "I had long since learned that men who pursue you to the dressing room are best avoided."[115] This time, Denison's persistence persuaded Dorothy to meet him and stay in touch with him.

After the Riviera engagement, Dorothy was offered a role in producer Darryl Zanuck's film *Island in the Sun*. She had a full schedule before production got underway. First came Cuba. She broke attendance records at the San Souci club in Havana, where she was crowned honorary queen of the Carnaval. Next, she was off to London to perform at the Savoy, where Prince Philip and Princess Margaret were among her admirers. She visited Oxford University and was again crowned, this time as Queen of May. Then it was off to Paris to meet with producers to discuss French film roles. Dorothy returned home exhausted, fell into a funk, and sought extensive therapy, and Preminger bought her a new house on Evanview Drive in the Hollywood hills.[116] Denison made a trip to Los Angeles to visit her, and she started making secret trips to Las Vegas to see him.

Filming began on the movie *Island in the Sun* in Granada in October 1956 before it eventually shifted to Barbados and London. In between, Dorothy snuck in a trip to New York to see Denison. The plot of *Island in the Sun* revolved around two interracial relationships, but Dorothy was not satisfied with inaccuracies in her character, particularly the fact that the West Indies woman would have been unconcerned with prejudicial implications of an interracial love affair. Dorothy was able to convince the director to make some changes, and though passionate embraces are depicted, the characters stop short of kissing on the lips.[117] The film later opened to

---

[113] Ibid., 335.
[114] Bogle, 342.
[115] Dandridge and Conrad, 197.
[116] Bogle, 345-347.

lukewarm reviews, but it earned a healthy profit.[118]

After *Island in the Sun* filming wrapped, Dorothy again returned home exhausted. She canceled several club dates and focused on settling into her lush new home. Her income reflected her status, and like many others in her social circle, she optimistically began investing heavily in oil drilling operations.[119]

Next on Dorothy's professional agenda was the film *Tamango*. Wardrobe fittings were scheduled in Paris, and filming was slated for the Cote d'Azur in the French Riviera in April 1957. Dorothy stayed at the sumptuous Hotel du Cap-Eden-Roc on the Mediterranean coast in Cap d'Antibes, and she dazzled the European press as she had during her visit to Cannes. She attended glittering galas with eminent stars, including Elizabeth Taylor and Monaco's Prince Rainier and Princess Grace.[120] After filming wrapped, the press discovered that Dorothy's journey home included a layover in Copenhagen, where Harold Nichols was appearing. The press set up a photo op, and the couple smiled and happily chatted for the cameras.[121] Dorothy again returned home exhausted.[122]

That summer, Dorothy testified in the bizarre and far-flung libel case against the celebrity gossip tabloid *Confidential*. Dorothy's testimony involved the magazine's story that alleged a sexual encounter between Dorothy and a random white man she met in the woods near Lake Tahoe.[123] Legal proceedings ended in a mistrial, but Dorothy was vindicated when the magazine was ordered to print a retraction and pay her a $10,000 settlement.

Around this time, Dorothy's manager Earl Mills contends that Dorothy told him she was pregnant with Preminger's baby. When Preminger would not marry her, Dorothy ended the relationship, and Mills says he made arrangements for her to have an abortion. "It was performed by a prominent doctor that I took her to in Beverly Hills,"[124] Mills claimed. "Having an abortion upset her for a long, long time."[125]

However, Dorothy's friend Geri emphatically denies Mills' contention.[126] Dorothy later wrote in her autobiography, "I asked Otto to give me a child. He said no. I should have gone on and

---

[117] Ibid., 360-366.

[118] Ibid., 382, 387.

[119] Ibid., 368, 372.

[120] Ibid., 380-382.

[121] Ibid., 388.

[122] *Tamango* became a smash hit that broke box office records in England, Spain, and France. Its subject matter led to distribution issues in the United States, where the film didn't open until August 1959. It had a short and unremarkable run.

[123] Bogle, 373-375.

[124] Ibid., 377.

[125] Mills, 156.

[126] Bogle, 377.

had that child anyway. I wanted a child. I should have had his child and made myself talked about, exclusive, and controversial."[127] Whatever the case, with Preminger out of her life, Dorothy saw Denison more often.

Dorothy's next role was in *The Decks Ran Red*, a low-budget project that filmed in Catalina in February 1958. The most notable aspect of the otherwise forgettable film was the scene in which white actor Stuart Whitman's character forces a kiss on Dorothy's character. It was the first interracial kiss portrayed in a Hollywood film.[128]

By the time filming wrapped, the long-rumored film version of the musical *Porgy and Bess* was becoming a reality. The project was deemed problematic because the story, written in the 1920s, was overrun with dated stereotypes that insulted members of the equal-rights-era black community. One advocacy group even discouraged black performers from appearing in the film. Producer Samuel Goldwyn wanted Dorothy and Harry Belafonte in the lead roles, but Belafonte refused. Dorothy had some harsh facts to face: her signature *Carmen Jones* had filmed a full four years earlier, and Dorothy wasn't getting any younger. "I decided that if Goldwyn was dead set on doing the picture, he might as well do it with me," she said.[129] Sidney Poitier was cast in place of Belafonte. Sammy Davis, Jr., Pearl Bailey, Diahann Carroll, and Dorothy's friend Joel Fluellen were also cast.[130]

Preproduction for *Porgy and Bess* commenced under the direction of Rouben Mamoulian. Sets were built, costumes were designed and fabricated, and a dress rehearsal was scheduled for 9:00 a.m. on July 2, but early that morning, the entire stage, with all the sets, props, costumes, and notes, was destroyed in a mysterious fire. Goldwyn rallied the cast and crew, and production work resumed, but significant creative differences arose between Goldwyn and Mamoulian, so Goldwyn fired him.

Goldwyn replaced Mamoulian with none other than Otto Preminger,[131] and during filming, Preminger viciously attacked Dorothy's acting. He screamed and insulted her and called her names. Dorothy, defenseless, fell apart. One co-star recalled, "He took delight in destroying her because she'd just crumble." Fluellen took it upon himself to help Dorothy keep herself together.[132] Preminger's abuse wasn't limited to Dorothy, as he lashed out at all of the actors. Soon they had enough, and during one of Dorothy's days off, they met with Preminger and demanded that he treat them all—especially Dorothy—better.[133] The nightmare only ended when filming wrapped

[127] Dandridge and Conrad, 192.
[128] Bogle, 404.
[129] Ibid., 400.
[130] Ibid., 394-398.
[131] Ibid., 409.
[132] Ibid., 413-414, 418.
[133] Ibid., 420.

on December 16.[134]

Meanwhile, Dorothy continuing seeing Denison, who had since moved to Los Angeles. As she put it, "I had someone. I needed someone so badly…Something in me cried out for a husband, for marriage, a home…I wanted to be in the backdrops of some man's life. I wanted a home life, and not to have to bat around the country in hotels for the rest of my life…"[135] Soon he convinced Dorothy to invest $150,000 in a restaurant he took over. In the midst of *Porgy and Bess* filming, a reporter noticed Dorothy was wearing a diamond ring on her left ring finger. "Oh, that's to keep the wolves away," Dorothy explained dismissively. Also dismissive were most critics regarding *The Decks Ran Red*, which opened in October. Preminger was even less kind. He told Dorothy on set, "You were rotten in that."[136]

Dorothy's friends were suspicious of Denison's motives, and they couldn't understand what attracted her to him. They felt he had no status, wealth, charm, knowledge, or even wit to bring to the table, and they viewed him as sleazy, crafty, and contemptible. For his part, Denison told a reporter, "I would definitely want her to quit her career if we married. I believe the value she would receive in having a husband and devoted lover would more than compensate for what she would lose by giving up show business." He knew it was just what Dorothy wanted, so she believed him.[137]

In March 1959, Dorothy and Denison announced their engagement. She was weary of traveling, had no desire to return to the nightclub scene, and was eager to settle down, but she left for London to film *Malaga* the next day. *Malaga* told the story of two traitorous jewel thieves. Dorothy played Gianna, who falls in love with one of the thieves, played by Trevor Howard. Again, Dorothy felt the character lacked depth, so much so that director László Bendeck couldn't even tell her what nationality Gianna was. Yet again, the film's interracial romance stops short of a kiss, but Dorothy stayed with the project because she needed the work. During filming, she continued relying on pills to sleep at night and to wake up in the morning, and she maintained her habit of keeping to herself, even when filming shifted to Spain's Costa del Sol. Upon release, reaction to *Malaga* from critics and audiences alike was tepid.[138]

Dorothy and Denison were married in Los Angeles on June 23, 1959, in a simple, un-Hollywood-like ceremony. Dorothy took sedatives to help her get through the day, and Geri served as Dorothy's matron of honor despite her opposition to the marriage. The newlyweds were immediately off to New York for the next night's *Porgy and Bess* premiere, complete with all the show business frills and flourishes. Again, Dorothy relied on medication to relax.[139]

---

[134] Ibid., 423.

[135] Dandridge and Conrad, 198.

[136] Bogle, 421.

[137] Ibid., 425-427.

[138] Ibid., 430-431, 444.

Reviews of the movie were mixed, but most critics agreed that Dorothy was far too elegant and refined to convincingly portray a tramp like Bess.[140]

The day after the premiere, the newlyweds flew back across the country to San Francisco for their honeymoon. Dorothy finally wanted to rest, but her new husband had other plans. He complained to Dorothy that his nightclub was on the brink of failure, and he threatened to jump out the window if she didn't commit to singing there. Furious, she shouted at him to jump. She ruefully pointed out that "the note on which we started our honeymoon was a banknote."

In September, Dorothy opened at Denison's outdated little nightclub. She was nervous, and he didn't know how to handle her. The reviews were poor, people stopped coming, and Dorothy's star power was irreversibly tarnished. No producer would seek his next leading lady at some downtrodden nightclub. In the entertainment world, appearances are everything, and Dorothy appeared down and out. When friends came to see her, it was obvious to them that something was personally wrong, and Denison tried to keep her friends away from her.[141]

East Coast audiences still wanted more of Dorothy. She appeared several times on the Ed Sullivan Show, and she returned to the Waldorf Astoria's Empire Room in February 1960. Engagements in Puerto Rico, Reno, Mexico, and Brazil followed.[142] Between stops, she bought a new home a bit further up the Hollywood hills on Viewsite Terrace. Denison had long been verbally abusive, but soon his assaults turned physical, and once those began, he turned quite vicious. Dorothy turned to champagne and occasionally vodka to numb herself. [143]

At this point, Dorothy didn't want to work anymore, but she had no choice. Early in 1961, Dorothy opened her engagement at Chicago's Palmer House Hotel with a disappointing performance. Later that year, she rebooted her nightclub act as the Dorothy Dandridge All Star Revue, complete with two male dancers, four male backup singers, an accompanist, a director, a choreographer, and elaborate costumes. The act appeared at venues in California and on a cruise ship. That fall, Dorothy filmed a guest appearance in an episode of the television drama *Cain's Hundred*. During filming, Dorothy missed her call at the studio one morning, so the director and an assistant went to her home to check on her. She had taken pills and locked herself in the bathroom. She wasn't incapacitated, but she needed the day off to recover. Dorothy also performed three songs in the episode that aired on NBC in February 1962.[144]

Shortly after that, production finally began on the ambitious, long-awaited film *Marco Polo*, set to film throughout Europe and Asia. Dorothy was cast as an East Indian princess, and she

[139] Ibid., 448-449.

[140] Ibid., 450.

[141] Bogle, 458-460.

[142] Ibid., 465-467.

[143] Ibid., 472.

[144] Ibid., 479-480.

flew to Belgrade, India, and Lebanon to film sequences.[145]

A picture of Dorothy and Alaine Delon in *La Fabuleuse Aventure de Marco Polo*

That summer, Dorothy was quietly hospitalized for exhaustion, but later, she was cast in a regional theater production of *West Side Story*. After two weeks of 14-hour-a-day rehearsals, Dorothy was spent before the play even opened. She only lasted a few days before she collapsed in the theater's parking lot and was temporarily removed from the production.

Back home, Denison's nightclub had failed,[146] and he was angry that Dorothy wasn't working.[147] The arguments and abuse escalated, and finally, Dorothy had enough. She told Denison to leave, and that she wanted a divorce. He simply laughed at her and turned even meaner. He raged

---

[145] Marco Polo was never finished. Film from the project was found to be uneditable, and the producer shot himself to death (Bogle, 484).

[146] Dandridge and Conrad, 208.

[147] Bogle, 488.

through the house and destroyed Dorothy's beautiful china and crystal. He pawned her jewelry, and he became more physically abusive.[148]

Dorothy's show had to go on. In October, she left for an eight-day Palm Springs engagement, but not before she filed for divorce on the grounds of extreme cruelty. She also obtained a restraining order against Denison and insisted that he must be out of the house before she returned. Denison slunk back to Las Vegas, lying to the press on his way out of Los Angeles.[149]

Dorothy was down, but she wasn't out, at least not until she learned that the oil investments she'd been making for the past three years were a scam. She had been pouring several thousands of dollars a month into the operation, and it was all gone.[150] Next, the Internal Revenue Service came knocking for a significant payment of back taxes.[151] Then, six hours before the fact, she learned her house was going to be foreclosed on. Geri and her husband paid Dorothy's moving bill and rented her a smaller home.[152] She later relocated to an apartment.[153]

In late March 1963, Dorothy filed for bankruptcy. She owed 77 creditors a total of $127,994.90. The day after Dorothy's court hearing, Helen Calhoun sent word that Dorothy would have to make alternate arrangements for the care of her daughter Lynn. Dorothy missed two months of payments to the woman who had been caring for Lynn for the past 10 years. Lynn, then 19, didn't know her mother. She only wept and pounded on the piano. Harold's mother helped out briefly, but soon Dorothy returned to court to surrender her parental rights. Lynn then became a ward of the state and was placed in the Camarillo State Mental Hospital.

Dorothy coped by drinking more champagne and increasing her consumption of pills, among them Benzedrine, Dexamil, Dexedrine, appetite suppressants, thyroid pills, and digitalis.[154] With Denison out of her life, Dorothy briefly dated film writer and producer Abby Mann. He socialized with Hollywood's elite, but the relationship didn't last because Dorothy felt she didn't belong in such circles anymore.

In July 1963, Dorothy appeared on *The Mike Douglas Show* to talk frankly about Lynn and mental health. *Jet* magazine called the appearance the "best thing that Miss Dandridge had ever done for an audience."[155]

Dorothy reconciled with former manager Earl Mills, who remained optimistic about Dorothy's

---

[148] Ibid., 492.
[149] Ibid., 494-495.
[150] Dandridge and Conrad, 7-11.
[151] Bogle, 498.
[152] Ibid., 500-501.
[153] Ibid., 519.
[154] Ibid., 506.
[155] Ibid., 512-513.

future.[156] She was booked for some minor appearances, but her drinking and anxiety threatened to cut some engagements short. Drunk, high, or lost in fantasy, she called friends and acquaintances at strange hours and talked endlessly or sang. She signed a contract to write an autobiography with author Earl Conrad, who Geri called "a dreadful, dreadful man." Mills later said that much of the book, titled *Everything and Nothing*, was "a mishmash of fact and fantasy."[157]

After Dorothy was hospitalized for anemia, Mills went with her to Rancho La Puerta, a health and fitness spa resort in Mexico. The visit was rejuvenating enough that Dorothy fulfilled engagements in Puerto Rico, Tokyo, and Mexico. She also returned to Las Vegas to see Harold and Fayard Nicholas, who were performing together again.

Fayard noticed right away that Dorothy wasn't herself. She was taking a lot of pills, and she seemed acting numb and preoccupied. Later, Harold wanted to take Dorothy out, but she didn't want to go, so he left her crying in her hotel room. The next day the three met at a restaurant, but Harold quickly left to play golf. It was too much for Dorothy, who flew home.[158]

Mills and Joe Glaser booked multiple minor appearances, but more promising, a film producer in Mexico wanted to discuss a project with Dorothy. With a comeback apparently underway, Dorothy cut down on her drinking and started working out again at a gym. On September 3, she tripped on the gym stairs and turned her ankle. The next day she and Mills were off to Mexico, where she signed a deal for two movies. Her foot was still hurting when she got home, so she went to the hospital. An x-ray confirmed a fracture, so a doctor told her to return the next morning to have the break set and a cast applied. She was worried about how the cast would affect her next engagement, and she didn't sleep well that night.

The next morning, Dorothy asked Mills to postpone her doctor's appointment. She said she'd be fine after a bit more sleep. After he called her several times and got no answer, Mills went to her apartment. When she didn't answer the door, he tried to open it with his key, but it was chained. Now alarmed, he got his tire iron from his car and broke the door chain.

When he finally got into the room, Mills discovered Dorothy lying dead on the bathroom floor.[159] At first, it was reported that Dorothy died of a blood clot caused by her fractured foot, but in November, a toxicological analysis concluded that she died of an overdose of Tofranil, an antidepressant. Later, a team of three psychiatric consultants conducted interviews with Dorothy's friends and associates regarding her emotional state leading up to the time of her death. This "psychological autopsy" concluded that her death was a "probable accident." For her part, Geri remained convinced that Dorothy committed suicide.[160]

---

[156] Mills, 225.
[157] Bogle, 520, 525-529.
[158] Ibid., 537-540.
[159] Ibid., 546.

According to Dorothy's wishes, her body was cremated, and her ashes were interred at Forest Lawn Memorial Park in Glendale, California.

The Hollywood Reporter published this touching tribute: "Yeats might have written it for tragic Dorothy Dandridge: 'But is there any comfort to be found? Man is in love and loves what vanishes, what more is there to say?'...Rest in Peace, Dorothy."[161]

Dorothy was posthumously honored with a star on the Hollywood Walk of Fame in 1983. Her mother Ruby died in 1987 and was buried next to her. Her father Cyril passed away in 1989, and her sister Vivian died in 1991. Since Dorothy's daughter was institutionalized as a ward of the state, there are few details about her life. Some online sources claim she passed away in 2003. If she is still alive, Harolyn would turn 77 in September 2020.

In 1999, the title role in the HBO film *Introducing Dorothy Dandridge* was played by Halle Berry. Fans and critics alike marveled at both the physical and professional similarities between Berry and the late star. "Many of her issues felt familiar to me, being issues I have been dealing with in my own life," Berry said. "It fascinated me that somebody could have so much and yet never feel really happy. It became almost therapy as it made me realize that this cannot happen to me, that her story can never be my story."[162] In 2001, when Berry became the first black woman to win an Academy Award for Best Actress, she dedicated the award to "Dorothy Dandridge, Lena Horne, Diahann Carroll. It's for the women that stand beside me...and it's for every nameless, faceless woman of color that now has a chance, because the door tonight has been opened."

Dorothy helped open that door, but she was fully aware it was not her destiny to walk through it: "Subtly, while experiencing what seemed to be a full acceptance, I encountered not-yetness...Whites weren't quite ready for full acceptance even of me, purportedly beautiful, passable, acceptable, talented, called by the critics every superlative in the lexicon employed for a talented and beautiful woman. Yet the barrier was there."[163]

Online Resources

Other books about Hollywood's history by Charles River Editors

Other books about Dandridge on Amazon

Further Reading

Best Actress presentation at the 1955 Academy Awards, youtube.com, accessed January 28,

---

[160] Ibid., 551-552.
[161] Ibid., 547.
[162] Mills, 214.
[163] Ibid., 165.

2020.

Bogle, Donald. *Dorothy Dandridge: A Biography*. New York: Amistad Press, Inc., 1997.

Cronin, Mary Elizabeth. "Vivian Dandridge, Singer With Sister, Dorothy, Dies." *The Seattle Times*, Nov. 2, 1991. archive.seattletimes.com, accessed Jan. 8, 2020.

Dandridge, Dorothy, and Conrad, Earl. *Everything and Nothing: The Dorothy Dandridge Tragedy*. New York: HarperCollins Publishers, 2000 [1970].

Mills, Earl. *Dorothy Dandridge: An Intimate Biography of Hollywood's First Major Black Film Star*. Los Angeles: Holloway House Publishing Company, 1999 [1970].

The Nicholas Brothers: We Sing and We Dance, An A&E Biographic Production, 1992. Accessed January 15, 2020.

Perito, Nick. *I Just Happened to be There: Making Music with the Stars*. Bloomington, Indiana: Xlibris Corporation, 2004.

Regester, Charlene B. *African American Actresses: The Struggle for Visibility, 1900-1960*. Bloomington, Indiana: Indiana University Press, 2010.

Valis-Hill, Constance. *Brotherhood in Rhythm: The Jazz Tap Dancing of the Nicholas Brothers*. New York: Cooper Square Press, 2002.

Free Books by Charles River Editors

We have brand new titles available for free most days of the week. To see which of our titles are currently free, <u>click on this link</u>.

Discounted Books by Charles River Editors

We have titles at a discount price of just 99 cents everyday. To see which of our titles are currently 99 cents, click on this link.

Made in the USA
Middletown, DE
15 October 2023

40876459R00024